MICHELANGELO

by Diane Stanley

HARPERCOLLINSPUBLISHERS

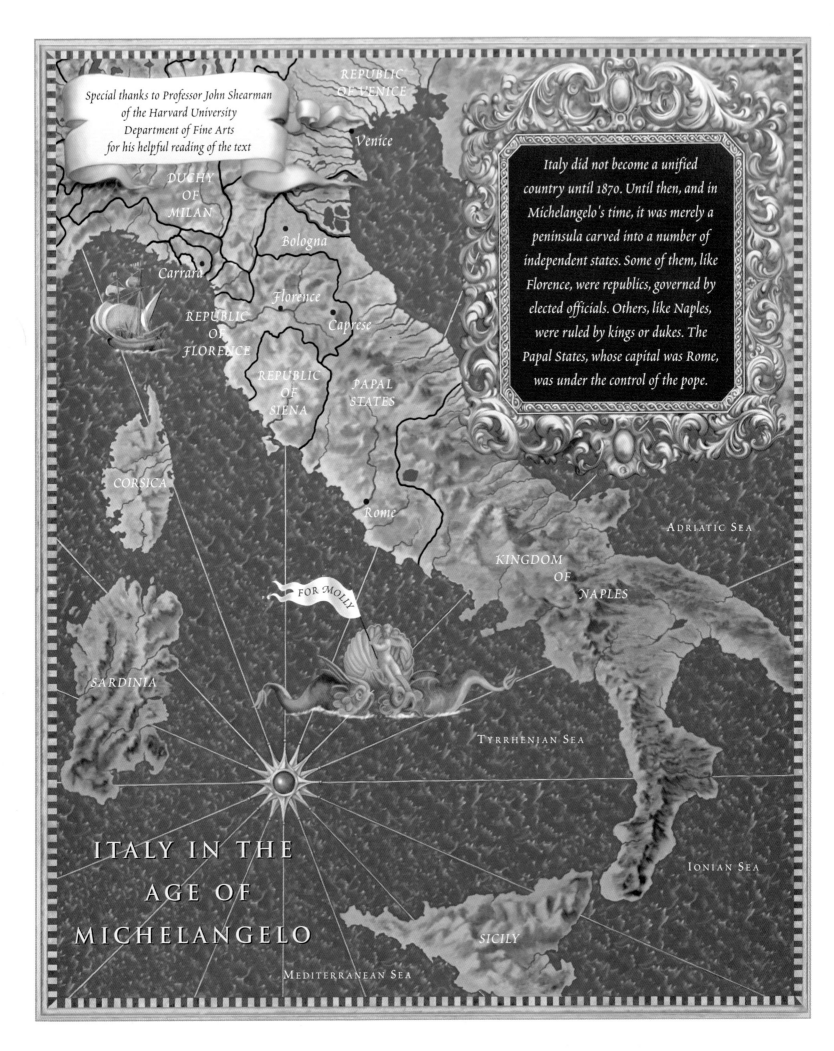

Special thanks to Professor John Shearman
of the Harvard University
Department of Fine Arts
for his helpful reading of the text

REPUBLIC
OF VENICE

Venice

DUCHY
OF
MILAN

Bologna

Carrara

Florence

REPUBLIC
OF
FLORENCE

Caprese

REPUBLIC
OF
SIENA

PAPAL
STATES

Italy did not become a unified
country until 1870. Until then, and in
Michelangelo's time, it was merely a
peninsula carved into a number of
independent states. Some of them, like
Florence, were republics, governed by
elected officials. Others, like Naples,
were ruled by kings or dukes. The
Papal States, whose capital was Rome,
was under the control of the pope.

CORSICA

Rome

ADRIATIC SEA

KINGDOM
OF
NAPLES

FOR MOLLY

SARDINIA

TYRRHENIAN SEA

IONIAN SEA

ITALY IN THE
AGE OF
MICHELANGELO

SICILY

MEDITERRANEAN SEA

IF MICHELANGELO had lived in some other time or some other place, he might never have become an artist. But as fate would have it, he was born in the midst of the greatest flowering of the arts in the history of Europe, an age we call the Renaissance. The name comes from the French word for "rebirth," and it refers to a time, at the end of the Middle Ages, when people began to rediscover the great achievements of their ancient past. This remarkable reawakening of learning and creativity lasted for about two hundred years, from the fourteenth to the sixteenth centuries. Though the Renaissance spread all over Europe, it was born in Italy, where magnificent Roman ruins were constantly being unearthed in fields and vineyards and at construction sites. The discovery of those ancient buildings, as well as masterpieces of antique sculpture and Greek and Roman writings on science and philosophy, inspired a whole new way of thinking and a whole new kind of art.

The very heart of Renaissance art was in Florence. By Michelangelo's time, the city had become a living museum, with masterpieces of painting and sculpture almost everywhere you turned—on the walls of churches and monasteries and in the public squares. Though there were talented artists in other places—in Venice and Rome and Siena, for instance— the very greatest came from Florence. The city had already produced Giotto, Donatello, Botticelli, Leonardo da Vinci, and many, many others.

The reputation of Florence as a place where artists grew like wildflowers after a summer rain is demonstrated by the following story, which may or may not be true. A certain young sculptor is said to have created a statue in the Greek style that he then buried in the ground to make it look old. He sold it as an antique to a Roman art dealer who in turn sold it to a wealthy art collector. When it eventually dawned on the collector that he had been cheated, he hired an agent to find out who the artist might be, not out of anger, but out of curiosity. It seemed to him that anyone who could make a fake that convincing must be every bit as good a sculptor as the ancient Greeks. So where did he tell the agent to begin the search? It was obvious to him that anyone that skilled would have to be from Florence.

And, of course, he was right. He traced the statue to Michelangelo, who would one day be judged the very greatest of all the great artists Florence ever produced. He would tower over the last years of the Renaissance, not merely shining in one of the arts—painting, sculpture, or architecture—but mastering all three.

ODOVICO BUONARROTI was a proud man from a respectable old family. He owned a house in Florence and had a little farm in the country. But for the past few generations, things had been going downhill for the Buonarroti family. They weren't exactly poor, but they had to be very careful with their money. And since Lodovico thought himself too refined to do ordinary work, they went on living in genteel poverty, waiting for something to turn up that was sufficiently respectable for a man of his status. Thus Lodovico was greatly pleased when, in 1474, he was offered a temporary post as court magistrate.

The job wasn't in Florence, however, but in the little village of Caprese, in a wild and mountainous region fifty miles east of the city. Late in the autumn of that year, he set out on horseback, accompanied by his pregnant wife, Francesca, and their young son, Lionardo. The journey took them several days, winding up steep and twisting roads into the mountains. There they moved into the small stone house provided for visiting magistrates.

It was in that house, in the early morning hours of March 6, 1475, that their second son was born. They named him Michelangelo di Lodovico di Lionardo di Buonarroti Simoni. He was to become famous simply as Michelangelo.

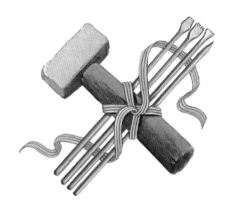

Stonecutter's tools

Michelangelo did not return to Florence with his family when Lodovico's term of office was over. Instead, his parents left him with a hired nurse in a little country town near their farm. It was a stonecutter's village, and the nurse was a stonecutter's wife. And so it was that the infant Michelangelo fell asleep to the odd lullaby of chisel striking stone. Years later he remarked that his love of sculpture must have come to him along with his foster mother's milk.

At some point in his baby years, Michelangelo was brought home to Florence. But when he was six, his mother died, and once again he went to live among the stonecutters. By then he was old enough to try his hand at the hammer and chisel. It is likely that someone gave him lessons in carving stone, for only a few years later, when he first began working as a sculptor's apprentice, he already seemed to know how.

Michelangelo was ten years old when his father, having recently remarried, brought him back to Florence and enrolled him in a grammar school. The education he got there—reading, penmanship, and a bit of Latin—was meant to prepare him for life as a gentleman. But Michelangelo, who spent all of his free time drawing on every scrap of paper he could find, had very different plans for his future.

Michelangelo had a neighbor, an older boy named Francesco, who was an artist's apprentice. Seeing that Michelangelo had great talent and a true passion for art, Francesco began bringing home drawings for his friend to study and taking him to visit the workshop of his master, the famous painter Domenico Ghirlandaio.

Frieze from a fresco in the Church of Santa Maria Novella

When Michelangelo was thirteen, he asked his father's permission to quit school and become an artist's apprentice, like Francesco. Lodovico was outraged. How could Michelangelo, the son of a gentleman, choose such a low occupation? Artists worked with their hands, after all, like common laborers. Lodovico tried beating some sense into the boy, but Michelangelo would not give up. Finally, in April 1488, he was apprenticed to Ghirlandaio for a period of three years.

Though he was just a beginner, Michelangelo soon found himself working along with Ghirlandaio's other apprentices on the most important commission of their master's career—a cycle of fresco paintings in the church of Santa Maria Novella.

The technique for painting in fresco, which means "fresh" in Italian, is very difficult. It involves applying water-based paint to wet plaster. The two elements are bound together in the drying process, so that the colors remain fresh and true even after hundreds of years. But the artist must work fast, and since the plaster usually dries in about six hours—depending on the weather—he must do his painting in sections, each small enough to complete in one day.

It was the apprentices, of course, who applied the plaster. They also made the brushes and mixed the paints and transferred the outlines of the master's full-sized drawing, called a cartoon, to the wall. This they did by rubbing charcoal dust through tiny holes pricked along the outlines of the cartoon. Only when everything was ready would Ghirlandaio pick up his brush. Even then he painted only the important parts. Everything else—including whole pictures that were too high up on the wall to see very well—was done by his assistants.

Michelangelo had only one year to learn the art of fresco painting from Ghirlandaio. Then the course of his life was suddenly changed by the most powerful man in Florence.

Lorenzo de' Medici, known to all of Florence as Lorenzo the Magnificent, was the heir to an enormous banking fortune. And though he held no government office, Lorenzo ruled Florence from his elegant palace, just as his father and grandfather had before him. Of the three men, all able rulers, Lorenzo was surely the greatest. He was a brilliant, generous, educated man with the sensitivity of a poet and the instincts of a true statesman.

Lorenzo loved art and had a fine collection of Greek and Roman sculptures on display in a private garden. It was a shame, Lorenzo thought as he admired his antiques, that nobody in Florence could make statues like that anymore. Then he had an idea. He would start a special school for sculptors right there in the Medici gardens. He hired an elderly sculptor named Bertoldo, who had once studied with the great Donatello, to be the master. In rounding up pupils for his new venture, Lorenzo asked Ghirlandaio to recommend a couple of his boys. The two he picked were Francesco and Michelangelo.

Bertoldo taught his new pupils to make figures in clay, then cast them in bronze. But this technique never interested Michelangelo. He was determined to work in marble, as the Greeks and Romans had, even if that meant learning on his own. Judging by the two beautiful carvings that he made in those first years, he does not seem to have needed much help.

Perhaps it was just as well that Michelangelo worked by himself most of the time, for he didn't have a gift for making friends. He quickly alienated his fellow apprentices with his scornful manner, especially a hot-tempered boy named Torrigiano. On one occasion, Michelangelo made a remark that pushed the boy over the edge. "Clenching my fist," Torrigiano recalled later with relish, "I gave him such a punch on the nose that I felt the bone and cartilage crush like a biscuit."

Michelangelo hadn't been all that handsome before the fight. Now he was forever after marked with the crumpled nose of a prizefighter.

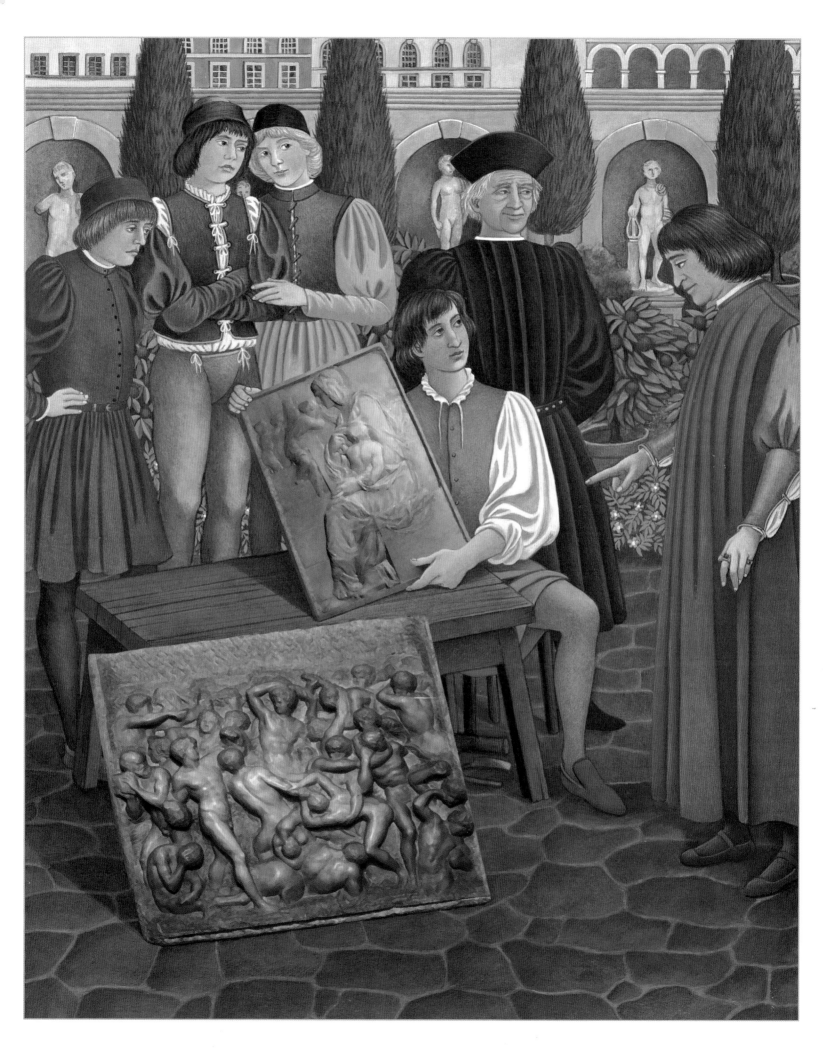

One day Lorenzo asked Michelangelo to run and fetch his father. It seems that Lorenzo had taken notice of the boy's unusual talent and, wishing to encourage him, had an extraordinary proposal to make. He wanted Michelangelo to move into the palace and live there as his son, to be educated along with the Medici children. He would give the boy an allowance and dress him in fashionable clothes—a purple cloak was mentioned. Lorenzo even offered to find a respectable position for the father. Naturally Lodovico agreed.

And so, at a most impressionable age, Michelangelo was suddenly thrown into the midst of the Medici circle, where poetry, science, philosophy, and art were subjects of dinner-table conversation, and guests included the most famous and brilliant men of the time. It was then that Michelangelo first began writing down his deepest thoughts in the form of poetry, something he would do for the rest of his life.

His schoolmates included Lorenzo's three sons, whose varying characters their father once described by saying that the oldest boy, Piero, was foolish; the middle one, Giovanni, was clever; and the youngest, Giuliano, was good. There was another boy living at the palace as well, young Giulio, the son of Lorenzo's beloved brother who had been assassinated by a rival family about ten years before.

What the aristocratic young Medici thought of the sculptor's apprentice, who now shared their schoolroom and was shown such favor, is uncertain. But the fact that these five boys should have grown up together is rather stunning, for all but one of them would go on to play significant roles on the world's stage. Both the "clever" Giovanni and his cousin Giulio would someday rise to the supreme position in the Catholic Church as Popes Leo X and Clement VII. "Foolish" Piero would succeed his father as ruler of Florence, though disastrously. And then, of course, there was Michelangelo, who would surpass them all. He would one day be regarded as the greatest artist of all time.

In April 1492, just a few months before his fellow Italian Christopher Columbus set sail from Spain and found a New World, Lorenzo de' Medici died. What caused his death is unclear, but he was probably not helped by the medicine his doctor gave him—a potion

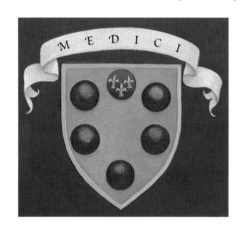

of crushed pearls and precious gems. The following morning the unfortunate doctor was discovered lying at the bottom of a well.

Michelangelo, deeply saddened by Lorenzo's death, moved back into his father's house. He was rather at loose ends at that point, for he was no longer an apprentice and had no desire to set up a workshop of his own. But he did need to bring in money for the family, especially since his older brother, Lionardo, had become a monk and could

no longer help out financially. As the second-oldest son, Michelangelo became the bread-winner for his father and two younger brothers, a role he would play for the rest of his life.

He began work on his first large sculpture, a figure of Hercules, which he eventually sold to a wealthy Florentine family. Michelangelo chose to portray his Hercules as the ancient Greeks and Romans had, in the nude. Michelangelo did not find the naked body in the least embarrassing, for he had been taught that man was created in the image of God.

It was the human form, in fact, that most interested Michelangelo as an artist. To understand his subject better, Michelangelo went to the hospital of Santo Spirito and got permission to study anatomy in the morgue. He spent hours there dissecting bodies, memorizing the origins and insertions of the muscles, the positions of tendons and veins. It was a gruesome exercise, taking apart the dead to discover their secrets. But it was there that he gained his astonishing power to bring forth life from a block of stone.

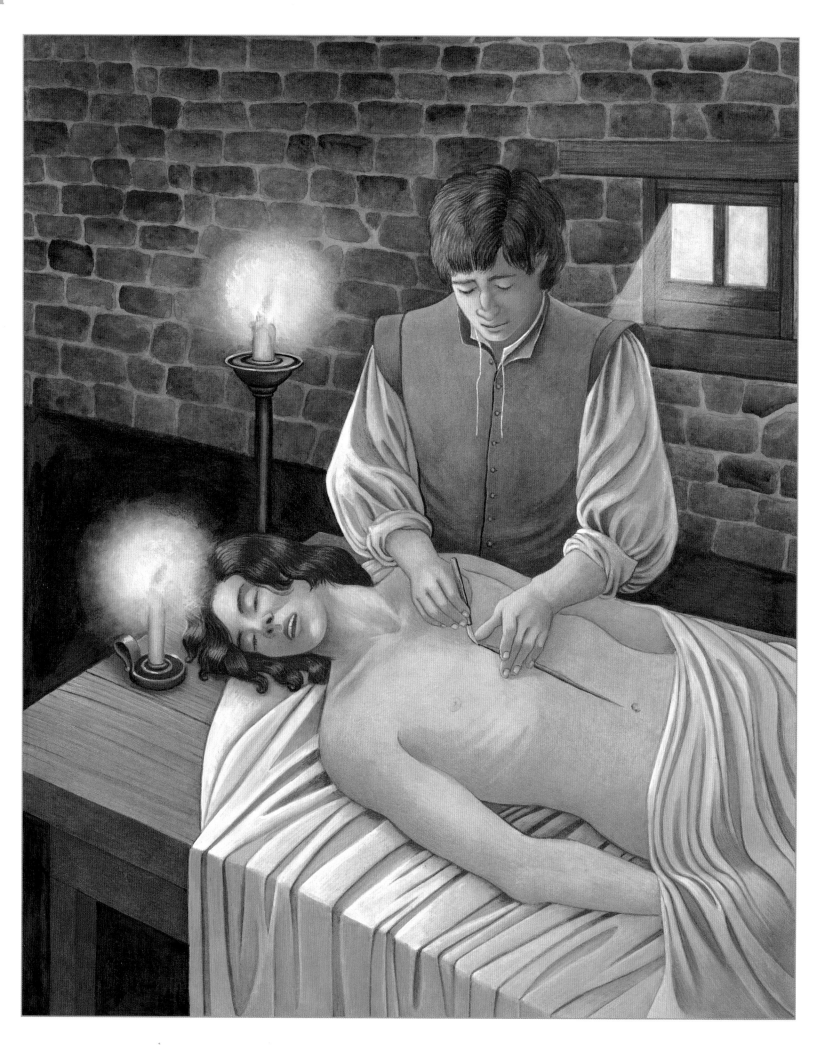

Upon the death of Lorenzo de' Medici, his son Piero came to power. Unfortunately for Florence, he proved to be as brash and arrogant and incompetent as his father had been measured, modest, and wise. Piero managed to offend just about everybody, had a knack for making bad decisions, and was completely unfit to cope with the serious problems that Florence now faced. His most memorable act as a patron of the arts was typical for its frivolity: On the occasion of an unusually heavy snowfall, he summoned Michelangelo to the palace to make a snowman!

The people of Florence began calling him Piero the Unfortunate and muttering under their breath about revolution. When the city fathers actually barred the council doors against him, it dawned on Piero that he had lost his position as "first citizen" and soon might lose his life. He hurried away from Florence by night, and on the following day mobs looted the palace.

Michelangelo was not there to see the tragic end of the sixty-year Medici rule. Afraid that his own association with the family might put him in danger, he had already left the city. He went first to Venice, then to Bologna, where he stayed for more than a year.

When Michelangelo returned to Florence, he found things greatly changed. The city had fallen under the spell of a fire-breathing religious extremist, the monk Savonarola. His doomsday sermons had reduced the people to a state of "terror, alarm, sobbing, and tears." The luxury-loving citizens of Florence were so desperate to save their souls that they brought out their most prized belongings—rich brocades, ornaments, antique books, works of art—and heaped them up in the public square to be burned. This was called the "bonfires of the vanities."

SAVONAROLA

With the people of Florence busy seeking salvation by burning their beautiful things, there was little for artists to do. So once again Michelangelo left the city, this time heading south for Rome. And it was there, only two years later, that he met the man who would make him famous.

This was an elderly French cardinal, soon to retire and return to France. He had lived for many years in Rome and had come to love it. He yearned to leave behind some beautiful monument in honor of the time he spent there.

Michelangelo came highly recommended, so the cardinal commissioned him to make a marble sculpture of the Virgin Mary holding the dead Christ in her arms. Such a scene is called a pietà, which means "pity" in Italian.

According to the contract he signed, Michelangelo was supposed to finish the sculpture in a year, but it took him two. By then the Frenchman had died, never to know what an amazing gift he had given the world. For when Michelangelo had finally chiseled every last fold of the Virgin's robe, rendered the veins and tendons in Jesus' hands so that they looked more real than real, and polished the marble to a high finish, the people of Rome were stupefied. Not since the time of the ancient Greeks had there been a sculptor with such amazing skill. And he was only twenty-five years old!

It was the Holy Year, 1500, the end of the century. Pilgrims from all over Europe flocked to Rome, where they heard about the astonishing new *Pietà*. Though some people remarked that Mary looked awfully young to be the mother of a grown man, the sculpture won almost unanimous praise. Thus, Michelangelo was annoyed when he overheard a man informing the admiring crowd that the *Pietà* was the work of a certain artist from Milan. The next night Michelangelo returned to the chapel with his tools. On the band that runs diagonally across the Virgin's chest, in beautiful Roman letters he carved his name.

MICHAEL·AGLVS·BONAROTVS·FLOEN·FACEBAT

Michelangelo Buonarroti from Florence made this.

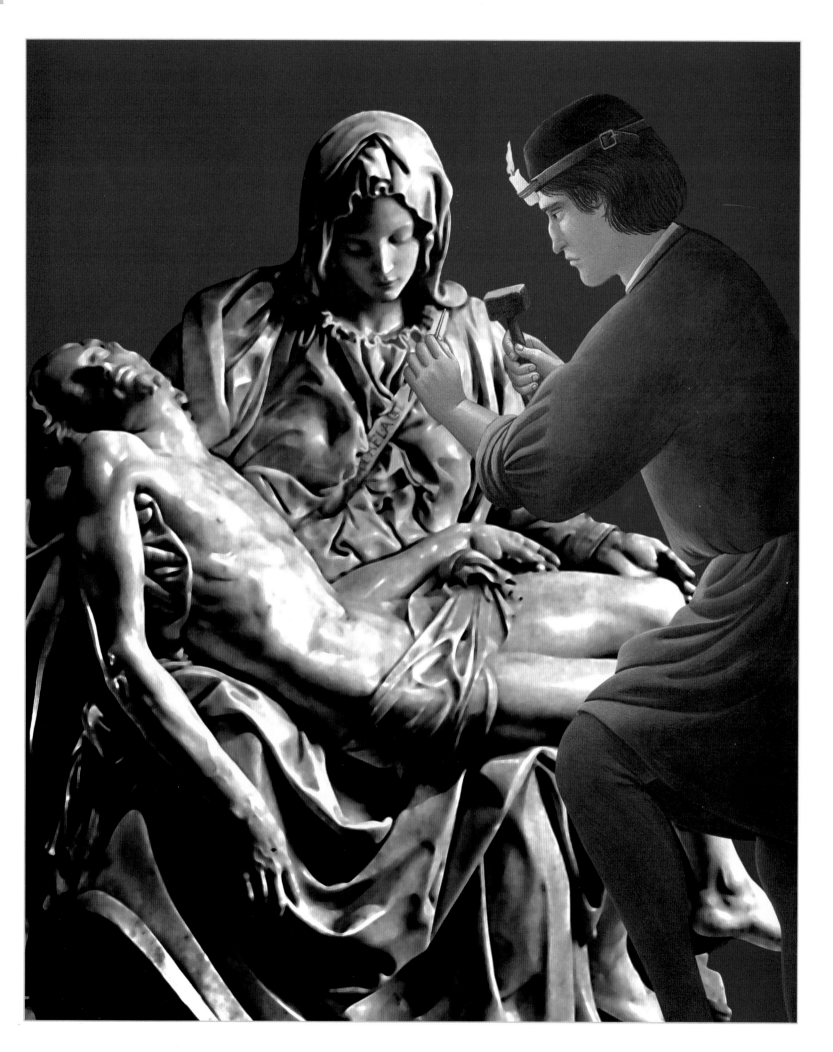

During the years he was in Rome, Michelangelo's friends wrote to him with news from Florence. Things were changing for the better, they told him. Savonarola was gone, having made the fatal mistake of charging the pope with corruption. The pope had struck back, accusing Savonarola of heresy, for which charge the monk was executed in the public square, on the very spot where he had once held his "bonfires of the vanities." The people of Florence, no longer under the dictatorship of the Medici or the madman, were free to govern themselves.

That was good news for artists. The newly elected government was eager to commission great works of art to glorify the city. One of those projects involved an enormous block of marble, affectionately named the Giant, which had been sitting in the work yard of the cathedral of Florence for over thirty years. It had been abandoned by an earlier sculptor who had blocked it out poorly, and since that time no one had known what to do with it. Now the city fathers were hoping to find a sculptor who could make something beautiful out of the misshapen block. Michelangelo knew he was the man they were looking for.

He returned to Florence and went before the cathedral board with his proposal. He probably showed them a drawing or a small clay model so they could see what his sculpture would look like. They were evidently impressed, because a short time later they announced that the Giant was his. A shed was built around the great block, so he could work in privacy, and on September 13, 1501, he began.

Michelangelo had chosen the perfect subject to show off his remarkable skills—the young David, in a moment of intense concentration, about to do battle with Goliath. He stands, resting on one leg, the other bent slightly. It is a pose out of ancient Greek sculpture, natural and graceful. Michelangelo knew his anatomy so well that his David is astonishingly real—except that he is seventeen feet high and blessed with godlike beauty. This, of course, was exactly what Michelangelo intended: David's physical perfection was merely the outward sign of his inner state of grace.

Michelangelo was already famous for his *Pietà*. The *David* established him as the greatest sculptor in all of Italy.

Success has its price. From that time on, Michelangelo would be hounded by patrons. Such superhuman labors would be required of him that he would later write, "Painting and sculpture have ruined me. . . . It would have been better if in my youth I had hired myself out to make sulfur matches!"

He was now asked to make "twelve larger-than-life apostles for the cathedral, to be delivered at a rate of one a year." That was in addition to several projects he had already taken on. With enough work to keep him busy for a good fifteen years, Michelangelo now accepted yet another major commission: to paint an enormous mural on one wall of the new council chamber. This was rather out of his line, for though artists in those days were expected to be skilled in every branch of the arts, he considered himself a sculptor. What little he knew of painting in fresco he had learned in that single year of apprenticeship with Ghirlandaio fifteen years before.

Leonardo da Vinci

But how could he turn the job down? Not only was it a tremendous honor to be chosen, but there was also the matter of the other wall, which was to be painted by the only man in Italy to rival him in fame, a man he both envied and disliked—Leonardo da Vinci. It was well known that Leonardo considered sculpture, which was messy and noisy, to be inferior to painting, which he thought more refined. It would be a real pleasure to beat the old man at his own game.

The people of Florence called it the Battle of the Titans and waited with breathless excitement to see what the artists would do. The council had asked them to depict military victories from the history of Florence, so Leonardo, who drew horses beautifully, chose a cavalry charge. Michelangelo was best at the human figure, so he picked a scene in which a group of Florentine soldiers had been surprised while bathing in the river.

People traveled from all over Italy just to look at the beautiful cartoons. But today, if you go to Florence and enter the council chamber, you will not find any paintings by Leonardo da Vinci or Michelangelo. Though Leonardo got as far as the painting stage, he used an untried new technique in place of the traditional fresco, and it failed. Eventually the picture was painted over. Michelangelo never even got that far before he was called back to Rome by the pope, Julius II.

Julius was a bold and ambitious man. What he wanted from Michelangelo was a monumental tomb, something that would carry his memory on through the ages. Michelangelo, who also tended to think big, sketched a colossal, freestanding monument of marble, more than thirty-six feet high, holding forty statues—all of them larger than life. Julius loved it, but he couldn't imagine where he could put such a thing. It would have to go in a very large church indeed. This set him to thinking of tearing down the old St. Peter's, the great mother church of the Catholic faith, built by the emperor Constantine more than a thousand years before. He would replace it with a new St. Peter's, one so big and so splendid it would be the marvel of the world.

At that time, ancient Roman sculptures were often unearthed by workmen digging around the city. Julius had quite a collection of them. One day Michelangelo was at the house of his friend, the architect Sangallo, when a message came from the pope. Julius wanted them to go and see what had just been discovered among the ruins of the emperor Nero's Golden House. Hurrying to the spot, they were stunned by what they found. "It is the *Laocoön* mentioned by Pliny!" Sangallo cried. Indeed, they were looking at the very sculpture described by the ancient writer as the greatest sculpture ever made. It had been lost since the time of the Roman Empire.

The three figures, the Trojan priest Laocoön and his two sons, writhed frantically in a death struggle with terrible serpents. Michelangelo was amazed by the beautiful technique and perfect understanding of anatomy. But what impressed him most was the extraordinary sense of movement. How very different it was from the calm elegance of his *David* and *Pietà*!

Inspired by this "miracle of sculpture," Michelangelo now threw himself excitedly into his work on the tomb. It is probably just as well that he did not know, when he first began on that great project, how dearly it would cost him—that it would haunt him for forty years, tarnish his reputation, break his spirit, and cast a shadow over his old age. His biographer Condivi called it the "tragedy of the tomb."

Michelangelo was a perfectionist, and for such an important commission he wanted only the best marble. So he went to Carrara, famous for its marble since Roman times, and stayed there for eight months "with two helpers and a horse and no provision other than food," to supervise the stonecutting. Julius had paid him a certain amount of money in advance, and this Michelangelo used to buy the stone and have it shipped to Rome. But there were additional expenses that came out of his own pocket. He had, for example, hired several apprentices from Florence to work with him on the tomb, and they had to be paid. He had to buy beds and chairs and other things for the apprentices and did so assuming that Julius would pay him back.

Then, with no warning, the pope dropped the project, announcing that he would not "spend another copper on stones." Julius had been persuaded that it would be bad luck to build his tomb during his lifetime—an idea that Michelangelo believed had been planted by a rival artist, the pope's architect, Donato Bramante. The presumed motive was to divert more of the pope's money toward his own great commission—for Bramante had been chosen to build the new St. Peter's—and away from buying marble for the tomb.

Though Michelangelo had lost his job, at least he expected to be paid. So he went to see Julius day after day, and each time was told to come back later. On the fifth visit he wasn't even allowed to see the pope but was sent away by a servant.

Beside himself with rage, Michelangelo rushed home, quickly arranged to sell his furniture, then wrote the following letter to the pope: "Most Blessed Father, I have this morning been driven out of the palace on behalf of your Holiness, whence I wish you to understand that from now on, if you want me, you will seek me elsewhere than in Rome."

And then he left.

The pope sent five men-at-arms after Michelangelo, but by the time they reached him he had safely crossed the border into Florentine territory. Julius, a stubborn man, wanted Michelangelo back. He began sending letters to the council of Florence, demanding his return. After the third letter in seven months, the council begged Michelangelo to leave. "You've tried and tested the pope as not even the king of France would dare," they said. "We don't want to go to war with him over you."

This remark was not meant as a joke. Julius was known as the Warrior Pope, and he was at that very moment with his army in the city of Bologna, which he had just reconquered after a rebellion. And that is where, reluctantly, Michelangelo went to beg the pope's forgiveness.

Julius accepted his apology, then put him back to work—but not on the tomb, of course. The pope wanted him to cast a giant bronze statue of himself, an odious task for Michelangelo, who didn't do portraits and hated to work in bronze. When it was done, Julius called him back to Rome for an even more unpleasant job.

Michelangelo was to decorate the ceiling of a great chapel, named the Sistine after its builder, Pope Sixtus IV. It was a most important and holy place, for it was there that the cardinals convened for the solemn task of electing new popes. Its walls had already been beautifully decorated by a number of other artists—including Michelangelo's old master, Ghirlandaio. But the ceiling, painted pale blue with a pattern of gold stars, was not very interesting.

Michelangelo was disheartened by the very thought of this undertaking. He didn't really want to paint anything, most especially not a ceiling. This had to be Bramante's doing, Michelangelo thought, to set him a task that would cost little, take a long time, and be very uncomfortable, too. And since Michelangelo had so little experience in fresco painting, there was always the chance he would fail.

While the workers set up the scaffolding in the chapel and plastered over the existing decoration, Michelangelo began planning his general design. Once he had a scheme he was pleased with, he began sketching the individual scenes and figures in detail. Though he often used live models for this, he also liked to make little figures out of wax or clay—he was a sculptor, after all—so he could study the way light fell upon the forms.

After about six months of preparation, Michelangelo was ready to get started. It was a very big ceiling—5,800 square feet—so he hired five assistants from Florence to help him paint it. But this arrangement didn't last long. He soon grew impatient with the assistants, who could not possibly live up to his standards, and sent them home. Their work can still be seen—clearly less skilled than Michelangelo's—in parts of the three panels depicting

the life of Noah. From that point on, using helpers for only the most mechanical and mindless tasks, Michelangelo proceeded to paint the rest of the ceiling by himself.

For the next four years, he spent all his waking hours more than sixty feet up in the air. He did not paint lying down, as many people believe, but standing in a most uncomfortable position. He even wrote a poem about it, illustrated with a little sketch. His back was bent like a bow, he said, his beard pointed toward heaven, and "my paintbrush all the day doth drop a rich mosaic on my face." He ate merely to keep his body going, nibbling on a piece of bread as he worked. At night he was so tired he would fall into bed "with his clothes on, even to the tall boots. . . . At certain seasons he kept these boots on for such a length of time that, when he drew them off, the skin came away together with the leather, like that of a sloughing snake."

He fretted constantly about money and had twice to go all the way to Bologna to ask the pope to pay him. To his brother he wrote, "I live here in great toil and great weariness of body, and have no friends of any kind and don't want any, and haven't the time to eat what I need." The painter Raphael, who both envied and admired Michelangelo, called him "lonely as a hangman."

Toward the end, Julius grew impatient for the ceiling to be finished. Perhaps he sensed the nearness of his own death and wanted to see the miracle that was in progress up there. Though he could climb the ladder to the top of the scaffolding and inspect the work up close, he wanted to see the whole thing spread out above him. "When will you finish?" he would ask again and again. "When I can" was always the answer. Finally, when Julius threatened to have the artist thrown from the scaffolding if he didn't stop painting, Michelangelo declared the ceiling finished.

On October 31, 1512, the chapel was opened to the public. They crowded inside, curious and excited, to see what Michelangelo had been doing up there for the last four years.

This is what they saw. Around the edge of the ceiling, he had painted the biblical ancestors of Jesus and dramatic scenes from the Bible. Between them were massive figures of the Hebrew prophets and pagan sibyls who foretold the coming of Christ. This frame of exquisite images led the eye up to the vast central space that stretched across the length of the chapel. Here, in nine separate panels, Michelangelo told the great biblical story of creation and destruction.

In the first three panels, God made the heavens and the earth. Then came the story of man, from the creation of Adam and Eve to the temptation by the serpent and expulsion from the Garden of Eden. The last three panels dealt with the life of Noah and the story of the Flood, balancing creation on one end with destruction on the other. Michelangelo had worked it out neatly so that the creation part of the ceiling rested over the altar, while the saga of human downfall rested over the heads of the people.

Michelangelo had painted the ceiling in reverse, starting with the Flood and ending with the separation of light from darkness. Halfway through, the scaffolding had been taken down and moved to the other half of the chapel, giving Michelangelo his first chance to view the work from ground level. As a result of what he saw, he approached the second half differently, making the figures much larger and the scenes simpler, so they are easier to see from a distance. His style changed, too, gradually becoming more confident and bold. To study the Sistine ceiling is to watch a genius learning how to paint.

Only four months later, Pope Julius died. The time had now arrived for Michelangelo to build his tomb. Though it had been four years since he had worked at sculpture, Michelangelo had been storing up ideas. While he was covering the Sistine ceiling with hundreds of marvelous figures in many dramatic poses, he imagined them in three dimensions. Now he would render them in marble.

He began by carving two captive slaves. They were meant to symbolize the arts, which at the death of Julius would lose their greatest patron and thus become "prisoners of death." With these two beautiful sculptures, Michelangelo had moved beyond mere perfection in anatomy. The figures seem to move and breathe, twisting dramatically, the legs turning in one direction, the torsos in another. This technique, used by the Greeks, is called contrapposto.

Next he made a seated *Moses*, so fierce and powerful, so full of energy, you half expect him to leap up from his throne and speak. He, too, was born in the Sistine Chapel, for he could easily be one of those massive prophets who had somehow managed to step off the ceiling and been magically turned to stone.

It is tempting to wonder what Michelangelo might have done next if he had continued. But instead, once again, he entered the service of the pope.

Rebellious slave

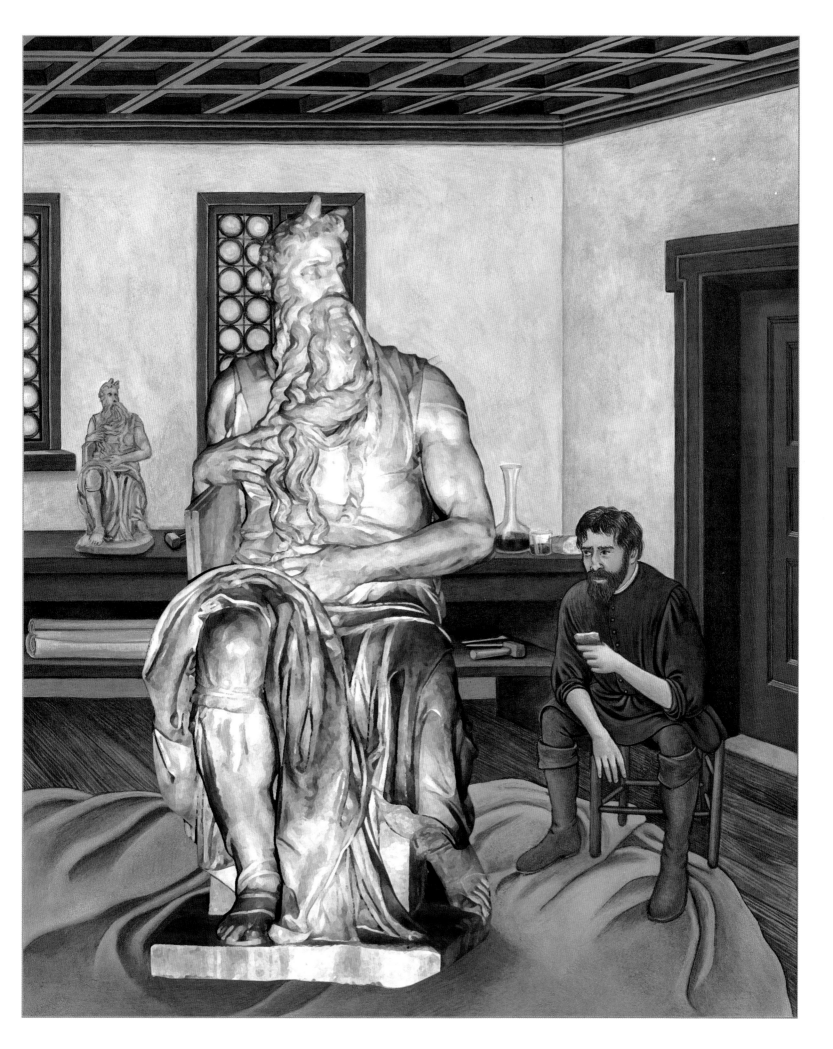

This new pope, Leo X, was no stranger to Michelangelo, being none other than his old schoolmate Giovanni de' Medici, the "clever" second son of Lorenzo the Magnificent. Giovanni had gotten an early start on his path to greatness. Thanks to Lorenzo's influence, he had been made an archbishop at the age of nine and a cardinal at thirteen, all leading toward this final promotion to the Supreme Head of the Catholic Church.

Since Leo was a Medici, one of the projects that naturally occurred to him was the decoration of the unfinished front of his family's church, San Lorenzo, in Florence. Michelangelo submitted a design for the new church façade, which was readily accepted. Then, insisting on complete control over the project, he went to the quarry to choose the marble.

Unfortunately, the pope insisted he use a new quarry, one that belonged to Florence. This caused endless delays, with the building of new roads to get the marble out and the blunders of untrained workmen. Michelangelo had spent the better part of three years there, "taming the mountains" as he called it, when the project was abruptly canceled.

He was stunned by the "enormous insult of having been brought here to execute the said work and then having it taken away from me." And, he added, "I still do not know why." Historians don't either, and to this day the front of the church of San Lorenzo is still unadorned.

Frieze from the Medici Chapel

The logical thing to do at that point would have been to go back to Rome and finish the tomb. Instead, Michelangelo agreed to remain in Florence and build the Medici Chapel, in which would lie the mortal remains of his old patron Lorenzo as well as those of his son and grandson. Later he was asked to design a beautiful library for the Medici collection of books and manuscripts. Michelangelo would work on these two projects, off and on, for the next thirteen years—through the sack of Rome, the fall of the Florentine Republic, the reign of two more popes, an epidemic of the plague, and the deaths of his father and his brother—and into his old age.

Popes came and went at a rapid pace in those days. Just as Michelangelo was starting work on the Medici Chapel, Pope Leo died. His successor lasted only two years, to be followed in turn by a second Medici pope, Lorenzo's nephew Giulio, who now became Clement VII.

His reign would not be an easy one. Just four years after his election, the army of Charles V, King of Spain and Holy Roman Emperor, marched into Rome. Many of the soldiers were Germans, followers of the new Protestant faith. They went wild with religious rage, burning and looting churches, turning the Sistine Chapel into a stable, and murdering priests and nuns and thousands of innocent citizens. By the time Pope Clement made peace with the emperor, Rome was in ashes and, in the opinion of many historians, the Renaissance was over.

Florence, too, was in turmoil. Taking advantage of Clement's weakness, the people once again threw out the Medici and established a republic. But the pope's weakness was only temporary, and it wasn't long before he was marching north with his army to take the city back.

The Florentines set to work repairing the city walls and planning their defense. It was common in those days for artists to work as military engineers (because they were trained in architecture), so Michelangelo was put in charge of the fortifications.

Soon he began to hear rumors among the soldiers that cast suspicion upon the loyalty of their commander-in-chief. Convinced that the rumors were true, Michelangelo went before the city council and denounced the man as a traitor. The council dismissed the idea as ridiculous, but word of his accusation quickly spread. One morning, as Michelangelo later told it, "a certain person came . . . where I was attending to the bastions and whispered in my ear that, if I meant to save my life, I must not stay in Florence. He . . . brought me horses and never left my side till he got me outside the city."

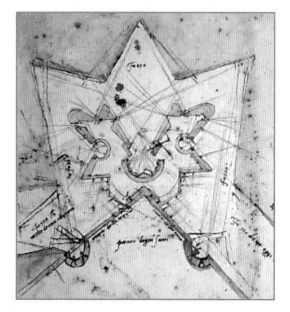

Michelangelo stayed away for two months. Only when his safety was assured did he return to Florence—just in time for a ten-month siege that ended in defeat. From that time on, Florence would be ruled by Medici dukes, never to be a republic again. It probably did not comfort Michelangelo to learn that he had been right. Their commander really was a traitor.

Michelangelo's plans for the fortifications

When he was almost sixty, Michelangelo left Florence for the last time. The Medici Chapel was still unfinished; the six marble sculptures he had managed to complete lay scattered about the room.

Michelangelo settled in Rome, where he hoped, once and for all, to finish Julius's tomb. But it was not to be. Pope Clement died, and his successor, Paul III, was eager to employ Michelangelo. When he tried to refuse, the pope lost his temper. "For thirty years I have wanted this," Paul thundered, "and now that I am pope, will you disappoint me?" And so once again Michelangelo set the tomb aside to paint a fresco in the Sistine Chapel.

This project had originally been conceived by Pope Clement, but Michelangelo had never gotten beyond the sketching stage. Now he began in earnest the enormous task of filling the entire back wall of the chapel—more than two thousand square feet—with a dramatic and chilling scene: the *Last Judgment*. High above the altar, Michelangelo

painted a wrathful Christ surrounded by saints and angels, his right arm upraised as if to smite the wicked. Below, bodies rise and fall in a furious swirl: the blessed pulled up from the earth toward heaven while hideous demons drag the sinners down into hell. Michelangelo even painted himself into the picture in a most gruesome way—his is the dark, distorted face on the flayed skin held by Saint Bartholomew.

The painting is so vivid and terrifying that when Pope Paul saw it, he fell to his knees and prayed for mercy. But others found it shocking. One of the pope's officials remarked that a picture with that many naked bodies in it belonged in a public house instead of the pope's chapel. Michelangelo was so annoyed by this comment that he painted the man into the picture—in hell, naturally. He is shown naked, with the ears of a donkey, in the grip of a hideous snake.

The censors won the battle in the end, though. Just a few years later, an artist was hired to cover the "shameful" parts with little draperies.

Michelangelo had always lived the life of a hermit. He did not care for fine food or clothes and sent most of his money back to Florence to support his father and brothers. Yet he seems to have done this more out of duty than affection. His letters home are all about business and money, with repeated complaints about how hard he is working to provide for the family. As he got older, Michelangelo grew suspicious and rude, coldly rejecting his nephew's gifts. He accused the poor boy of waiting greedily for him to die, hoping to inherit his money.

Nor had Michelangelo found companionship in marriage. "I already have a wife," he once said, "who is too much for me; one who keeps me unceasingly struggling on. It is my art, and my works are my children."

It is truly remarkable, then, that as he neared old age this lonely and tormented man should suddenly fall into the kind of deep and loving friendship that had eluded him all his life. And more amazing still, it happened not once but twice.

The first of these friendships was with Vittoria Colonna, a high-born widow of middle age. She was an intellectual, a noted poet, and a very refined and devout woman. She stirred his spirit and stimulated his mind. With Vittoria, as with no one else, he could speak of the solemn things that lay in the troubled heart of a man moving ever closer to the end of life. When Michelangelo was seventy, Vittoria Colonna died, leaving him despondent. He had lost, he wrote, "the great fire which burned and nourished me."

The other friendship was with Tommaso Cavalieri, a handsome young nobleman of great intelligence, grace, and kindness. He represented, for Michelangelo, the absolute ideal of human perfection. Michelangelo wrote ardent poems to Tommaso and gave him gifts of beautiful drawings. This devoted friendship lasted for more than thirty years, and when death came for Michelangelo, Tommaso was at his side.

St. Peter's Cathedral

In February 1545, the "tragedy of the tomb" finally came to an end with the official unveiling of the monument to Julius. The original design had been cut down to something small and manageable, with only three sculptures from Michelangelo's hand. Though one of them, the Moses, surely ranks among the greatest works of all time, still the tomb as a whole was disappointing. Michelangelo himself was ashamed of it—as apparently were the heirs of Julius, for the pope's bones lie elsewhere.

Michelangelo was then seventy years old and so famous that people were already summing up his accomplishments and considering his place in history. Every public figure has critics, and Michelangelo had his share, like the writer who complained that all of his figures were equally massive and muscular—men, women, and children alike. "Whoever sees one figure by Michelangelo," he wrote, "sees them all." To almost everyone else, though, he was the Divine Michelangelo, a living legend, the master of the Renaissance.

Yet old though he was, the crowning achievement of his remarkable life still lay ahead. In 1547, Pope Paul appointed him chief architect of St. Peter's.

It had been more than forty years since Bramante first began work on the new church, and construction had been going on all that time. To protect the tomb of St. Peter, over which the church was built, a miniature classical structure had been erected. Beyond that, very little had been accomplished, for after Bramante died, a string of architects followed, each changing the previous design and starting over again. Now this commission, the most important of the age, fell to Michelangelo.

He would work on St. Peter's for the rest of his life. When he was eighty-two, knowing that he would never live to see it finished, Michelangelo constructed a model of the great dome for the builders to follow. Even as he neared the age of ninety, Michelangelo still rode out to the site every day.

Old age is not easy for anyone. Most of Michelangelo's friends had died, and his health was beginning to fail. What sustained him then, more than anything else, was his daily work on St. Peter's, that miracle of architecture. And though he devoted the last seventeen years of his life to this task, Michelangelo refused to accept any payment. He said he did it for the good of his soul.

In his last years, he would still go into his studio sometimes and pick up his hammer and chisel. The vigor that once enabled him to "knock more chips out of the hardest marble in a quarter of an hour than three young masons could have done in an hour" was a thing of the past. Still, he went on working at his craft because it gave him pleasure. And it is fitting that he should end the cycle of his great works exactly as he began it—with a pietà. But this one he would not finish.

Shortly before his death, Michelangelo burned some of his poems, along with many of his drawings, sketches, and cartoons. Perhaps he didn't want anyone to see all the work that went into the creation of his finished paintings. Or maybe he was echoing those "bonfires of the vanities" from his youth, for by then his thoughts had begun to turn toward the next world and the salvation of his soul.

On February 18, 1564, feeling restless and feverish, Michelangelo sat down to make his will. He left his soul to God, his body to the earth, and his goods to his nearest relatives. To his friends, gathered to support him in his final hours, he spoke of how much he regretted "dying just as I am beginning to learn the alphabet of my profession." Then, shortly before five on a chilly winter afternoon, as he sat in a comfortable chair by the fire, Michelangelo died at the age of eighty-nine.

In an age of great artists, he was perhaps the greatest, creating immortal works in all three of the major arts—sculpture, painting, and architecture. Not even Leonardo da Vinci could match him in that. Yet near the end of his life, Michelangelo looked on those great works of art, to which he had devoted his life, as "of little value." But then, with a touch of pride, he added, "They will last for a while."

This they have certainly done.

BIBLIOGRAPHY

Brandes, Georg. *Michelangelo: His Life, His Times, His Era.* Translated by Heinz Norden. New York: Frederick Ungar Publishing Company, 1963.

Bull, George. *Michelangelo: A Biography.* New York: St. Martin's Press, 1995.

Buonarroti, Michelangelo. *Complete Poems and Selected Letters of Michelangelo.* Translated, with foreword and notes, by Creighton Gilbert. Edited, with biographical introduction, by Robert N. Linscott. Princeton, New Jersey: Princeton University Press, 1980.

Condivi, Ascanio. *The Life of Michelangelo.* Translated by Alice Sedgwick Wohl. Edited by Hellmut Wohl. Baton Rouge: Louisiana State University Press, 1976.

Coughlan, Robert, and the editors of Time-Life Books. *The World of Michelangelo, 1475–1564.* New York: Time-Life Books, 1966.

De Tolnay, Charles. *The Art and Thought of Michelangelo.* Translated by Nan Buranelli. New York: Pantheon Books, 1964.

De Vecchi, Pierluigi, ed. *The Sistine Chapel: A Glorious Restoration.* New York: Harry N. Abrams, 1992.

Gilbert, Creighton. *Michelangelo On and Off the Sistine Ceiling: Selected Essays.* New York: George Brazillier, 1994.

Goldscheider, Ludwig. *Michelangelo: Paintings, Sculptures, Architecture.* London: The Phaidon Press, 1964.

Hibbard, Howard. *Michelangelo.* New York: Harper & Row, 1974.

Vasari, Giorgio. *Lives of the Most Eminent Painters, Sculptors, and Architects.* Translated by Gaston DuC. De Vere. Introduction by Kenneth Clark. New York: Harry N. Abrams, 1979.

Wilde, Johannes. *Michelangelo: Six Lectures by Johannes Wilde.* Edited by John Shearman and Michael Hirst. Oxford, England: Clarendon Press, 1978.

The illustrations were prepared using watercolors, colored pencil, and gouache on Arches watercolor paper.
The images of Michelangelo's art were manipulated on the computer using Adobe Photoshop.
Book design by Diane Stanley and Kathleen Westray

Michelangelo
Copyright © 2000 by Diane Stanley
The photographic material on pages 32–33 and 41 is reproduced by permission of the Photo Vatican Museums.

Printed in Hong Kong by South China Printing Company (1988) Ltd.
All rights reserved.

www.harperchildrens.com

Library of Congress Cataloging-in-Publication Data
Stanley, Diane. Michelangelo / Diane Stanley. p. cm.
Summary: A biography of the Renaissance sculptor, painter, architect, and poet, well known for his work
on the Sistine Chapel and St. Peter's Cathedral in Rome.
ISBN 0-688-15085-3 (trade)—ISBN 0-688-15086-1 (library)
1. Michelangelo Buonarroti, 1475–1564—Juvenile literature. 2. Artists—Italy—Biography—Juvenile literature.
[1. Michelangelo Buonarroti, 1475–1564. 2. Artists.] Title. N6923.B9 S546 2000 709'.2—dc 21 [B] 99-52380

1 2 3 4 5 6 7 8 9 10

First Edition